*ZOOM*

Also by Susan Lewis:


*Heisenberg's Salon*
*This Visit*
*State of the Union*
*How to be Another*

# ZOOM

*Susan Lewis*

WINNER OF THE 2017 WASHINGTON PRIZE
Andrea Carter Brown, Series Editor

THE WORD WORKS
WASHINGTON, D.C.

*Zoom*

Author photograph by David Golove © 2017
Cover art by Brenda Goodman: "Untitled (a1)" (Detail),
Oil on Wood, 72" x 72", by Brenda Goodman © 2012
Cover Design: Susan Pearce Design

ISBN: 987-1-944585-18-1
LCCN: 2018931390

# ACKNOWLEDGMENTS

Thanks to Mark Bibbins, Krystal Languell, B.K. Fischer, Sam Witt, Patty Paine, Michael Boughn, rob mclennan, Trace Peterson, Richard Peabody, Lisa Marie Basile, Stu Watson, Alex Cigale, Halvard Johnson, Michael Whalen, Gillian Conoley, Dale Smith, and Carolyn Guinzio for first publishing earlier versions of the following poems in these anthologies and journals:

*The Awl*: "The Original Self-Pleasure Equation"
*Bone Bouquet*: "Monumentally Manumitted"
*Boston Review*: "Stolid," "All Signs," and "Dear Sir"
*Devouring the Green: Fear of a Human Planet: An Anthology of New Writing*: "Elsewhere," "Words Dying Off," and "Slipped Between"
*Diode*: "Until the Inevitable"
*Dispatches from the Poetry Wars*: "Drumming," "Make Haste," "Sweetie Pie," and "Uttered"
*Dusie Tuesday Poem*: "We Might"
*EOAGH*: "Silence, Wastrel," "Mind the Gap," and "Mouth My Idea"
*Gargoyle*: "Wandering"
*Luna Luna*: "Strait & Laced," "Stacked on His Head," and "Back at the Convocation of Lost Souls"
*Monday Night*: "False Promise" and "This Is When"
*Prelude*: "Everyone Agreed"
*Shadows of the Future, the Argotist Otherstream Anthology*: "By Which I Promise"
*Truck*: "There Is the Wear"
*Urgent Bards: An Urbantgarde Anthology*: "In the Puddles"
*VOLT*: "From the Outset" and "Another Chance"
*White Wall Review*: "Today the Leaves"
*Yew*: "Crashing" and "Stealing Upstream"

And thanks to Kristy Bowen and Jeffrey Side for first publishing several of these poems in the chapbooks *Some Assembly Required* (Dancing Girl Press, 2011) and *At Times Your Lines* (Argotist e-books, 2012).

My deepest gratitude to Series Editor Andrea Carter Brown, and to Nancy White, Karren Alenier, and everyone at The Word Works for their support and encouragement, and for the judgment, expertise, and energy they so cheerfully devoted to creating this book.

Heartfelt thanks, as well, to Brenda Goodman, for permitting me to adorn this cover with her magnificent artwork, and to Rae Armantrout, Ilya Kaminsky, and Maureen Seaton, for their generous praise.

And ever-more profound love and gratitude to David Golove, my partner in pretty much everything, for his wise and tireless devotion to supporting my writing life, in more ways than anyone could ever imagine.

# CONTENTS

# 1ST

...the sky is that splendor inside a man's head,
if his head is not, in fact, his own unique sky.

—José Saramago, *Baltasar and Blimunda*

I have learned to use my eyes and distrust them.

—Michael Palmer, "Notes for Echo Lake 11"

*3*RD

# EVERYONE AGREED

this was a thrilling catastrophe. There were
the usual photo-ops & spell-checked
swoons. Octopeds got the jump on the
rest of us, though their spread was useless
against the suck. Spare fur was exchanged
for sexual favors until the water fermented
& all hell broke loose. No one remembered
to access their 20:20 hindsight until
the razor light blinded us with its odor
of inferiority. There was anger & danger
beyond our wildest dreams, which stopped
flowering once the humdrum imploded,
divesting us of our history & its discontents.

# Back at the Convocation
## of Lost Souls

rejoicing was finally added to the ritualistic menu.
*We've got to hand it to you*, said the loyal to no
one too particular. By that time individuality
had become a problem in solution's clothing.
Most of the limbs knew not to carry on with
frostbitten tips & hypothetical protection. Yet
the lecture line stretched back & back, which
really hit home for those of us still stiff from
hobbling towards knowledge on hand-me-up stilts.
Meanwhile, the chattering of bones laid a phased
track for the fleet-footed innocents among us.
Regrettably, most of the prepared remarks were
overwrought, spilling thinly veiled spleen on the
eager descendants of our most favored mistakes.

# Make Haste,

or wander through the leaving gaze of caverns
miniscule to man. While ever & always this
sparrow & that legend slave. Corpuscle to kings
& silvered minstrel song. Lassitude of dogs
barking for their phantom herd. Or serenade
with brutal echo (location, location). She who
knows what Hecuba is to him. The good pagan
squirming in eternal tepitude, yearning for the
honest burn. Unless Mormon is the answer, a life
of licked dogs in jeweled cabins, cavernous egos
all the rage. Another masterpiece missed to pieces
by the lurid canons of yore. This wormy segment
divvied & conquered by the soiled honor of our
sullied humor, cut timely to the quick & the
dead, rolled high & mighty in their silken ardor.

# STOLID

as this lost house, vacancy immured in cryptic
walls. Underestimate this risk or die trying.
Slavering like angered bills, nestled between
some & none. Introductions like leaky cups, a
masquerade of sight. Hail to the cheat & other
icy escapades, indebted to begetting the microbes
haloing our dreams. Careful, in our slap-dash
way, like typewriter monkeys theeing & thouing
'til the vowels come roam. Standing in place,
aerobically enmeshed. Thrashed & slathered.
Illusion of stability mister & missed until baby
makes free. Heralded by our times to a fare-thee-
well, folded like angered proteins riding flotsam
brains. Like cows tipped & teetering, hale
fellows well set, madly stranded on this beached
& rolling rock, riding out its hurtled spin.

# All Signs

pointed to the same confusion. On the second Monday the third person persevered. Tiny toes like exclamation points, daffodils, or doubts. While the mistress of ceremonies sobbed off the opportunity to introduce her own death. Chanting, mutinous, the girls in our hearts danced on pins & needles, stalking expired goals. Souled like dreaming dogs: backwards sever, forward fever. Naysayers said their. Bed-layers lied. Mixed wintry standards dropped precipitously on the embryonic future poking its head from the earth's gut, while the spicy amongst us inverted our convolutions to the *nth* degree. Out-rhymed, intellect ceded the probabilistic navigation to instinct & its moody henchmen. Lolling yet again on shaky ground, the middle deliquesced to flab & folded.

# CRASHING

everybody's party like the losers we are born to be,
loosening of lip & hip, hyped to rip & ride until
we rot. *Répondez s'il vous plaît* with the sorrow of
a sorry excuse excusing the leaving self, the left
luggage of our botched baggage weighing the
way for those who go next (paired, unprepared).
Blind needing the blind in this clogged dance,
stumbling through our tunnel of narrow vision
to the fabled light blaring the approaching *fin*,
funneling our shrunken prospects to the tidal
*drip, drip, drip* of human seas, clouded by
sentiment as fleeting as the rest, while we panicked
pan-flashes brighten & ignite & even shine.

# WE MIGHT

think to pause redemption for a public service
pronouncement, jingling like a ring of keys.
Losers caged until restored to the belly of the
ball. Interruptions erupting in the fullness of
time, main-lined & eventful as kitten gifs or self-
amputation, imputations tragic as circus beasts
gamboling with counterfeit pleasure, sad layers
painted & latent, clowning past our timid hearts.
While laughter's double edges touch & mask what
we avoid. Blood splashed on winning screens
training innocents like trick ponies, appled by the
dubious, pushed to pony up reluctant rationales,
seen & raised, razed like doubts in the rush
from judgment. Uncompassed thought fired &
crisped, taking force for freedom until it takes us.

# Sunset in the Nursery,

soft-edged, like Play-Doh or consideration,
sauced in pastel colors, surging silently in the
strawberry light. While we look on in admiration
& despair. The obdurate sun setting. Setting the
date. Settling the score. Setting down the whys
& wherefores. Settling down to its line in the
proverbial sand. Settling into the distance, sending
us packing, sidling dutifully towards the pale
satellite offering her second-hand luminescence.
That one seems masculine & the other feminine
is just another sign of how far we haven't come.
While we whine like retrograde babies, shying
from the shadows, cracking our sealed lids &
waiting for the night to show us if & why &
how much we can grab before the curtain falls.

# ELSEWHERE

in this agglomeration of pixelated particles,
fanned by the cooling breeze, up to resolution,
high & mighty in its binary resolve. Toward
the sweet smell of excess, mechanically done
in. The ragged self tooled, cashed in to pop our
tempting bubble. Entanglement, entitlement, &
all that jazz. Like tail-feather, tailwind, backdraft,
backlash. Also ignition, that purposive miracle.
*By their claws shall we know them* & abhor
our native selves, abjure this vicious privilege.
Plus this violate outlook, its illusory blue, like
deity & other synthetic beauties. Still witnessed
by the insouciant clouds, accruing & divesting
any made indifference, hedged & bound.

# TODAY THE LEAVES

jostle for the sun's brandished meal. A minor chord day, compressing the worms in their tight & silent world. Reluctant seeds gaping to a care-worn future, scattered cosmos unimpressed. *What's that you say, Madame President?* Emoticons embellishing perception via harbingers of swoon. Elsewise processing the inputs, despite an endless weary trap seasoned with too much not enough. This standard deviation from deviation thrown at any problem like onions, gold nuggets, skyscrapers, & severed heads abloom with silken hares. Who might not be precious, messy, & inconsequent? Roped by the tinsel glint of agency, that floozy hope, or her closest uncloseted kin.

# In Praise of
# Miscommunication

& her co-star, depending. Trying not to stare at
the posterior pronation of their disregard. Which
might or might not be normal from an imaginary
point of view. That we have sampled many favors
& forfeited them all, distracted by these tentacles
probing the pockets of our work & play. How loudly
they purr while we watch & wait for intention to
be laudable. Until the real work begins, without
admitting hope for tomorrow or tipping off the
Sandman to the secret of our glandular success.
That we might endorse him & hang back where
the blossoming aborts in fits & starts. Which is
not to say fertilized so much as dug in & reaching.

*2ND*

# DEAR SIR

or Madam, until you lose your head or mother its shred, wrapped in mystery & mead. No levity for this, your skid life. No mercy while you bilk your betters, sent flying to spy on your attempts to rise. Across the deep there are many with nary a hook to hang on. While ever & anon those lads with rainbow limbs snake through the gloom. Another day another dolor. Not to mince woulds, but this sibilance is skilling us. While you who wish upon a stare — where would you turn & fleetly tumble? The Burning Dervish never knows whereof he'd speak, mute as he is, spinning in his vicious circle, boring his whole through our dank & dappled gaps.

# SILENCE, WASTREL,

cease & resist. While across the palm, microbes
frolic like atoms, attracted & repelled by
circumstantiality & the greater food, landed
& penetrant as the bluest eye or God's day
off. To halve & have again, heaving against
the universal grain, drastic & brandished
with blandishments of the highest order.
Muddled like coins, minted & intoxicant,
while info-bits slip by, corruptly fanciful,
tacking in the solar wind. Never fear the rest
of us — knottily petaled, lost & nautical,
rising from the death of for-&-against,
leaking color from our grayscale whole.

# UTTERED

& muttered by your animal lips, *sotto voce, in media res*. Ever & ever on offer *qua* blood tide, *qua* cellular divide, *qua* irruption cascade. Nodding agreement *sub silentio* & *sub rosa, nunc pro tunc* & *corpus ipsa loquitur*. Awash or not in chemicals of every hue & cry, massing at the borders of the self, clambering for a seat at the table or a turn at the proverbial wheel. Offering *mystery loves company* as if *intime* with that epochal ruptured membrane & the brutal drama launched, ticking the clock on the incubus chance to suck oxygen unstrained by blood. Whether it be nobler to breathe or surrender to the gentle susurrations of your erstwhile float. That tenuous chain of command plus lesser inducements trailing from cell to cell like trusty insurgents, relentless & compliant in expectant loss. Unhinged as all disciples, as devoutly to be feared.

# SWEETIE PIE,

managing your ruffled feet of frigid terra.
Minister to bad boy angels & their miscreant
moguls, spooning salvation into gawping
beastly beaks. While ever in abstraction
shall they reign or decohere. Like any royal
flash, measureless to slits allured. Faceted,
like crystal vapor glazing the world with
brilliant danger. Admired & middling blind,
touching your debutante tongue to its brittle
secret tale. This soft friction throbbing to
a flocked & regal trance, feathered voices
wooing us to feed the mothering soil.

# THE ORIGINAL
## SELF-PLEASURE EQUATION

& other inconsiderate lilies. Or any mineral aspiring to ambulate. Which is not to say living in close quarters. Leaves rubbing & rustling, promiscuous breeze egging them on. To carry on tastefully until the bitter end. To stay on the lookout for aught nubile in *négligée*. Not to be neglected like the young & juicy fancy their feelings (to the swell of strings). In other words America & its discontents, table of. Quantity, quality, & other mysterious divides. Yet another veiled Islamic reference. No rest for the wary. No wrest for the offended infidel smashing bottles on officious effigies. To be faithful & timid, to redirect resentment 'til it rolls over & submits. Remember what you never understood. Reciprocate. Fill the gaps with measured starts. Sprinkle with gestures rational & inapposite.

# Monumentally Manumitted,

rubbernecked & blubber-naked, the uncivil
war rages from top to toe. Floral notes topping
the lost & throbbing meat. Wannabe cyclones
circling like buzzards, issuing their carrion
cry & mustering an interest in anywho's
future. Matchless fine if passing estranged.
Misapprehension mastering the age of untruth,
unforgivably forgotten. Ministered to those
more or less consumed by miss & mister fortune.
Joined by the loving arms of this soldering iron
& that rusty stitch. While the bend in your
elbow rises to the tidal zone slapped by rock,
paper, wizard — a tribute to the breathless kick.
Don't pretend you know whereof you want,
distracted as who isn't by this spongy spectacle.

# In the Puddles

of your future: ruminants. *Ruminate on this,*
they say, while you marvel at the float of moths
spreading their pall of loss like the mad song of
lonely thugs. Who is not tickled by roots of their
own making? Entangled & confused with glass,
hopes, fur, El Niño, & unacknowledged drones?
No doubt there's a pixel for that. Hunkered face
to face with the cruelty of your victims. Who is
not matchless in their need & greed? Or another
salvage operation for these, our left souls. *Please
sir, won't you stay your hand?* & hum with the next
misery, wading on through the indifferent storm.

# Stacked on Your Head,

balancing like paperclips or tepid water, the
flutter of wings. In the midst of chaos, pain. In
the midst of pain, sympathy. In the chill of battle,
flashes of understanding, which may or may not
dissipate like curls of smoke, analog confusion, or
the gamble of the body on its vigor. Anonymous
monstrosity like the ego at the bottom of your
heart's closet. The whimper & screech of this
desire to be desired, mislaid memes mewling like
no tomorrow. A harrow holier than now, in which
our sore spots evade all biotics, pro & con, be they
ever so persuasive or G-forced, the faux-gravity
of our predicament notwithstanding so much as
super-glued to this great & ruined mother. Until
no one is amused by the newest cruelty. In the
event of collapse, submit or defy (according to
your genome & your angle of commitment). Not
to start from the beginning, ignoring the moaning
dark & its unbeautiful whirl. Who would not
applaud Milton's fury? Who would not trade their
sight for his? Not to deny the haunting odor of this
slow burn & its impassioned frills, thrilled as lips
hushing the known for sensation's coup — graceful,
explosive, or dreamy-sweet until loose-limbed we
load the lorries, discharge the canon, & grasp at
any drift & dwell until she's bound to drown.

# FALSE PROMISE

Someday, when all of this is over, & other parlor tricks. Like smoke to ash. Or ask & ask again. Sporting craftwork & roughened fingers, skin raveled & unraveled, a living shroud for lonely bones. Penelopes still, tough & stringy, lax in demand. Patience-blind, industry-*distrait*. Until a boat bobs on the beach to break this bungled beat. The ties that bine & wrap your neck like barber poles, bitters hopped & bothered, plus a head for days numbered to last until they don't. Bear up, sip the gist of aught that ales you, pale & wondering that *no birds sing*. Like mead to the measured temper, tempered to the point of melting, down & out of patience if not patently amused. Like JK's sparrow scratching out its message in the desiccated sedge. The virgin negatively capable as any gentle trickster dropping knights & wights like breadcrumbs to mislead the studious lost. Sacs of testosterone sapped by the succubus whispering *walk this way*, while the good girl waits & time stops & goes on gendered tracks.

# UNTIL THE INEVITABLE

may or may not transpire upon this bright,
screaming water, this cloudy contoured breath, this
lacerated need. While the Minions of Clarity
deny your best contentions & misericord mangles
your nose-ring of fire. Who else knows how
to credit envy's silk, spun so lushly from
our spindly limbs? Or prepare for Mistress
Ingenuity to cast a lucid glance on this necklace
of questions. While Mr. Valor invites you to the
Infinity Jamboree & Gomorrah languishes in the
wallows of herstory. But whence, you wonder,
sails Salubrity? — who won't stop keening for her
sweet & sour acolyte, moaning iambically in 3:4
time, dying for the glow of your remnant pulse.

# Stealing Upstream

to reach the beauty seed. Wanting for. Not riven
but licentiously taxed, need-struck, united.
Why not offer your infancy or plead guilty
as particulately charged? Lost as any battle.
Brittle & eventual, warrantless as sparrows
pecking, positively capable. Others not so savvy
or confused, eventful as lost breath, dangling
from this cliff & the next, aspirational &
in-. Out of order & dissed, inordinate & sub.
Uniformed in unformed cahoots, stepped out
from your martial peonage, spreading murk as
if it's what you live for. Meanwhile, back at the
heart of the convocation: miasma. Plus a bridal
train of pardon — wan, perhaps, but never
staunch. Coursing juice through unmapped
sylvan routes, nosing toward the seeping source.

# Basic Research

Perseverating; that is, digging for the logic in
this slow accretion. Realigned meaning best
intentioned to stop us in our tracks. Plus the
periodic table, to which we're not invited.
Through the murk, energy flowing to its mock-
toothed acolyte & victim. Beware the bump &
grind of this unctuous animal. Plus attraction
& repulsion, repulsive attraction & headlong
propulsion to the next bit, when butterflies sip
nectar & flash their extravagant dread-eye threads.
Run while you may or may not source the right
bauble, babbling as our lost world spins off toxins,
hurtling from the fraught unsought alternative.

# DIDDLING & DAWDLING

with woulds & worlds, ambi/valent towards
sweetness & bite, heavy & light, the gravity of
situations situated between nothing & something,
obscurity flirting with irrelevance, dancing nude
to its own persistence. Or envy the flashing
lights, the jingle to jangled ears, whose game may
or may not be over (*insert coin to continue*) —
no matter how tinny (to the point of tenacity)
— as narcissistic as mammon, the neat trick of
coveting immortality in anonymity, revolution
in allusion, illusory or illustrative as any stitch
in time or fashionably late. Right yourself by
borrowing your own invention. For best results,
baste an army or strike a match in 3:4 time
until it springs to life or its insidious nemesis.

# For Times like Now,

when the matter misbehaves, sending scrambled
signals. Components clashing like mismatched
mates. Bad favors flowing in currents, a currency
of missed discomfort. Wave if you want to go.
With the flow, for instance. With God or Her
designate. With grace, like a flower, inclined
towards the bright improbable. Coughing like a
ruminant startled by dark but distant prospects.
Choking on your borrowed cud. Strangled by
your thankless dodder, binding you, sucking
out your sallow juices & your nagging fear.
Cleansing you, rousing your blindered loyalty.

# Four Shortcuts to Amelioration

This is not about the headlines, although it can't hurt to check & double on a daily basis. Most likely double trouble, which is to say learning by (counter) example. A.k.a. muddling through, stopping to smell every Eureka & lemon slice. Going long to reach the nifty pith; triangulating. At times you're tempted to go round the bend because they know you're watching. Try knitting your brow or inhaling something spotty & dense. No harm no. Squawking like a cartoon geek. What an elitist would elect, spotting leaky fluids & leaking spotty fluids, viral & superfluous. Bled dry by tedium: day in, day in. *Only delegate*, you growl, lauding the lay of the landed, biding your ticked-off time.

# In a Contingency,

don't forget to map your lost rigidity. Real if not
ideal, salivating & slavering for a taste of any kind
of limit. Limned in profile or its loyal opposition.
Vaunted as any victor, marching towards Bethlehem
to be borne. Not to put too fine a point on this
erratic view to be personalized, with or without
divine flourish. Plus a cherry on top, cheery &
paternal as any daughtered god. Lest you wonder
how to map or tolerate this sojourn. In animal
years, a blink of the eye: a flash, a nod, a morsel, a
smithereen. A vale of saline exudations. A gobbet
in the receptacle. Long on fear. Short on *on*. Ask
anyone, ask everyone. There is the glow of lights at
evening, there is ecstasy in tasteless bursts, there is
the optional leave-taking with its captive blossoms,
scrambled attention, measured horror. After which
you may compound the error of your wayward
wondering (to the taut & tragic swell of strings).

# Righteous in Retreat,

thorns probe your yielding feet. A path like any other. A math that some might puncture, pleadingly. While here & there you blunder into sacrificial traps. Mouth objections. Eye benedictions, like so many cracked seeds. Pith sprouting willy-nilly from the lips of babes. As *en route* to the block you yield & yield against a neck beautiful & bent, a sensibility or a fenced stability, an inutility to reign in the attack. Going for the. An offering like any mother, wet & warm, holding back & gushing forth, rushing with the force of ages to an ageless innocent.

# ANOTHER CHANCE

for time to masquerade as something else. While tenths imprint like dogs on ducklings, teasing you in troops. Minor past fading & reiterate, wise & unwise as mini sugared reinforcements. Like the soulful loris, whittled by our auto love. Crutched by that selfie memory to limp & stumble. Or celebrate the march of Négritude towards the song of pouched motherhood & our love for thirsty worms. Listing to the left of enter, bent to touch the cheek of any golden issue, eye bright as water & random as the latest god. Meandering, the beauties, while you burnish their decay. Satisfaction chained or your honey sacked. Leading with amanuensis while the other balks, guiding your darling dewclaws through the dizzy loop of bygone days.

# IF / &

or any, which could be hordes, secreted perhaps, lorded over & scattered, aiding & abutting this edge, this easement, this *sine qua non* of communitarian dismay. No buts about what's strewn willy-nilly like snowflakes, like fallen leaves, like gum splats. *Only compress*, as many might propose, while the government insists you destroy yourself & obliging as ever, you oblige. In this way we neglect *noblesse oblige* & its naughty *Doppel, négligée*, despite or because of that tantalizing through-line swirling & scrolling round your peaky little points, tendrilling back to the nowhere we began, that universal end, in or out of conditional as the case may be & somewhat is (to the swell of strings).

# Either / Or

If & when. Else you suffer. Atop a mountain. Atop this mountain. To dive off. To sink or soar. You might hear them murmuring, you might take their interest as encouragement. Or something out of bounds. Amounting to leaves rustling, thighs rubbing, sex on stilts. The hills livening without recourse. Down, but not out. Clipped, but not cut off. One way is to laugh. By their levity shall ye know them. Another is more muscular. Extend & contract. Honk if you conflict, alone or in pairs. Listen in on the finches, working the room in epicycles, knowing more than they can ever know, blithely eschewing your not-to-be-trusted Late Bloomer's Special.

# IN PRAISE OF LYING

to yourself or others. Lying down & lying in, lie
in wait until you pounce. Starched & bothered.
Let this one go as unduly insightful or any kind
of threat. Like mythology, like fairytales, like
hired guns selling you on what you'll never
know. Comfortable as couches, couched in
pretty promises. Crouching, set to pounce or
animate the ones you jilt, waiting slack-jawed.
Or breathe, more or less than enough. Tense
& lunge. Or feed them promises & codicils,
take them for another ride, run them ragged.
Address another bar of evidence. Smile into
the grinning air. Temporize until they strike.
Buzz off 'til something vital tapers off or snaps.

# In Praise of Efficiency,

lolling beneath the surface: lissome, recombinant,
redolent of coffee, of crushed herbs & nematodes.
You know the ones. Entitling the trees, each
its own edifice, aflutter with raucous energy.
Not inclined to make a mark so much as add
their breath to the enabling stew. Not heat so
much as light or any flavored particle, wavering
improbably like all of us, here & gone & here
again like no tomorrow. Whistling Dixie, as the
genius famously feared. A weighty mess, blurred
& caloric as ne'er-do-wells spinning webs off of
webs: sexy grifters, purring as they lie in wait,
taking up our slack. Supping on your naive juices,
converting them to bright anterior schemes.

*1ST*

# DRUMMING

to your inner waltz I hesitate, halt of step &
runneth ever. While you hum & lean in fat
fragments, with no amount of legs to help you
stay the course. While misers save, spindrifts spin,
& lackadaisies loiter. Which in no way affects
our terminal arrangement, arriving & departing
every moment's frail & frantic quietude. Until
you are reminded to mind your inner child. Yes,
waltzing, on her restless, glassed-in toes. Pinched
& pennied, penuried 'til dearth do us part. Spun
like sugar or silken history, locked & bothered.
Never to consider the self, resigned to the ash heap
of mystery. Ought you dare or care? Displaying
the lost landscape of your nether license, craned
& cradled in a palm of your own breaking,
life line throbbing like any body's business.

# WORDS DYING OFF

like flies, lifestyles pixelating, records corrupted.
The fearful grasping at the lost. Like landline, snail
mail, Send Another Sad Emblem of dismissal.
Like slow & steady, states of being *sans* update
(as in *flown*, as in *clueless*, as in *chatter-starved*).
The obscure & the celebrated stuck on this
light-bouncing surface, Narcissi with or without
reinforcements & other major minor distinctions.
Buried in the distracted crowd, 'singing.' Neither
Berkeley nor Fossett can console. Come to me now,
admired as I am mired in my mineness, & ever &
ever my fantastic fifteen flee. While the universe
grows itself to death beneath our naveled gaze.
The wisdom of the infant processing to overload.
Never again to match that full-court press, toggled
with nectar & rebuke, illumination & deceit. The
trap of conscious self not yet sprung. After which
we ignore & are ignored, resist & are resisted,
eyeing the exceptions that prove the rule. Or
masturbate & masticate & ruminate on variations
on the same old themes (as in *purity of purpose*, as
in *for its own sake*). Which is to say large & small
undistinguished & indistinguishable, *face à face*
with the strange music in which criminals husband
executioners. What you might or might not do, as
if & until back drops forth & lingers, more or less.

# There Is the Wear

of thought that cuts & floats without blight or bile.
There is the fine particularity of subatomic particles.
There is the clouds' rosy hole through which
creation peeks & beckons, then retreats. As for the
frantic lives of animals & plants, the faux stillness
of minerals, the bell curve of phase change — I
am confident in osmosis, both cognitive & erotic.
I am certain of limits, as limitations litter my fear,
like plastic isles in a hapless green sea. You swallow
animal, mineral, & vegetal. Twenty questions bare
identities not yours, which slips & slides from
my desire like false advertising, false promise, or
truthful testimony. In the world of bats, dinner is
charted geometrically. In the world of foresight,
death has long tentacles, prying backwards, spoiling
some moments, enhancing others. Not to regret
sentience is to be ready for the next brutal blessing.

# THIS IS WHEN

you model your pet tricks, my fine, demonic muse.
Tainted & otherwise beg I, never choosy. What is
to be done but breathe in toxins & perseverate.
That is, follow our fearless leader, another aging
aunt with violet hair, violent if inviolate, cave-
bound. Or validate her quiver, sharp as sticks
with her poisoned pointers striking easy mark my
words, when I make them. When I make them fly.
Beyond good & other fairytales, be they Grimm
or gleaming in fool's micaceous glory, faux glam
like spam & cluttered, heart-clutched in banal
vanity while mass-hysterical pump-hyped hopeful
friends & Romans lend us their capitals, grand &
tawdry as Sukey or your favorite battered figment.

# Slipped Between

heat & gear, sheet & shear. Sheer as brilliance, unless murk glowing at the speed of virtue — lying with or lying in some simpler version, slick as silicon or a silken noose. The horror of no way to know. In this distance between psyches, viral phonemes flying like bird flu between lying swine. Though you google my veracity, I say unto you, verily: *hi-ho, Silver; que sera, sera.* It's best to whistle or sing lark-like while the clash of symbols deafens your tin ear. Until you're mostly whine & winner, keen to balance or teeter & fall for this *Sturm und Drang,* this testosterone storm mashing our ever-sensitive, analog globe.

# Strait & Laced,

layered like lashed cake, kindled with the
spark of genesis measureless to sand. Love-
bitten fleabag minstrel of loom, woven of
resistance & desire, slavering for a taste of.
In which the master is slave to mastery.
King of kings. Thing of things. The folly of
limbs & their shaky logic, unfired furnaces
of tainted clay. Tetched in the erogenous
head, by which I mean satisfy something
or die trying. The enemy grinning in our
prismatic hearts. Fingering the molecular
furnace, hot & bothered. Throbbing towards
correspondence, the irrepressible hope of fit.

# I Can't Say
# How We Got This Far

First I'm wading through daisies, nosing your
breath, then we're like this, not one way but its
opposite, in ever-more confusing rondo form.
That we fail doesn't mean we shouldn't try to
align ourselves, give or take reality's allowance.
Do you hear the crickets yelling at those hungry
birds? Do you smell the storm crackling in the
hollows? I've tossed petals at the lot of them, they
are not impressed. You would call me desperate,
& I would demur. I would call you Babyface,
or Salamander, or Mr. Critical, depending on
the stuck market & the relative humility. Now
there's sorrow raining down from the agitated
clouds. Perhaps they yearn for a more congenial
atmosphere. They, too, are underappreciated.
Meanwhile you've aced more mean feats, leaving
me jealous of my former self. Call it sweet-&-
sour grapes, call it no-strings-attached, either
way we might be sorry, & sometimes I am.
Other times I tremble for more of the same.

# In the Meantime,

like dancing rabbis or hen-pecked pigeons,
complicated. Gracile. Ambling with the melody.
Kiss me on the downbeat; show me your teeth.
Hum. When you flex this sentiment I remember
mostly everything. The babies riding on our
backs. The surf cooling our tails. How you loved
to ruffle my feathers. Another brand of passion
for another version of this swirling flesh. The way
you shoved your paws in your pockets, sleek as
sheets. Your thoughts might have lost me but
there's still one language only we can speak, if
ever atmospheric conditions favor us again. I can
wait if you can, until the balance sheet weighs
in with a wink or a nod or any kind of sign.

# ONLY DISSECT

Between rain & what it pounds, this gulf. Remote as gratitude loves resentment or any awkward pair. Neither me nor my shady *Doppel*, ganging up as ever on your inner emoticon. Like a rain shadow glowering with unsated appetite. While you bow daily to the deontological pressure via sympathetic scalpels, melodic lies, & optimistic pharmaceuticals, to name just a few of my favorite things. Don't worry, you'll have more lashes to succumb to, when they beckon. When you flaunt your cares & wares. Look around the womb. None of this is yours. Yet you will lose it, as surely as my aim is anything extrapolated from the evidence. Perhaps you lack the appetite for this tasty tangle. Perhaps you'd rather dance a *Tarantella* or pillage something virginal, original or no. Still your aversions crouch in the corner, waiting to pounce. *This is a job for everyone*, you never tire of reminding those who will & will not listen. But what should be the punch-line? How will we rebound when it clocks us on the chin? Who will glean the logic of our final iteration?

# First the Gleam & Glitter

of something dazzling yet murky as magic, a new idea or a new view. Unreal to you but never to me. In which one of us wrong, blind because unwilling, unwilling because afraid. One slippery reality mistaken for another. A beautiful boy with long legs & the possibility of emergence. This might mean intoxication or disorderly words, pigment or angle of light, clouds or a girl whose eyes smile no matter who looks into them. This might be a beauty to be earned. By which I mean a lesser horror withstood. Deny & ignore or return to square one, try again or never in this arid limbo, this craven how-to, this picking-apart, this *aha* of comprehension, this one-way tunneling to the hope of any other.

# At Times Your Lines

bring me to tears, on page & canvas brow. At
times I want to tongue your worry, trap &
release it to the wilderness. That round the heart
of things crouch shadows, like slaves struggling
from stones. I would cry *emancipator, free
thyself,* but that seat is taken. Consider Dante.
Consider the lilies, trailing death & taxes. Also
lingerie, opaque or sheer, depending on your
ideology & the prevailing winds. That nature
in her dalliance rides the vacuum — flirting,
like anyone, with her God-given limits. Not
to drown in the commonplace, its soporific
tides. Grasping at attraction to extrapolate.
Sprinkling the path with any sort of glean.
Leaning towards lips & their delicate admissions.

# Wandering,


unless you know what's good for. By *good* you might mean *covet*, & round & round like no tomorrow, when you could use a hug, or something stiffer. Share & share alike, meaning much to explain before the untimely end of this awkward juncture. Or send forth chains to clash & conquer. Harness logic or match the craft of thickened air & other secrets known or somewhat flown. By *known* you might mean *weighty beyond this flighty scale.* Or slay me sweetly with your stilettoed stalk, track my trials on this trail of tendered triumphs, trap me with your treacle treats. Why renounce or explain? Why wax & wane? When all is semblance & your temptress tricks more feeble flickers on the dusky wall.

# MIND THE GAP,

you intone, animal & vegetal as the crash
of waves or the hum of bees, ominous &
soothingly inscrutable. You can't fathom
how I want to want. Deafened by the din
of friction warming this corner of the vasty
chill. Until the katydids tire of their old saw,
busy with *he said, she said* 'til they cease,
pleasured & immured like leaf-green mirrors.
*I see you*, we want to say, propping our lids
with that tonic, discipline, views stretched &
twisted by variations on the same old theme.

# MOUTH MY IDEA

here, until your sympathy wields its secret
fury. Or match my cue to your rattling
throat, another slick saber for this mound of
toothsome treats. Later we will linger while
the dying light lets imitation bump & grind
her glowering gruel. Must salvation be a savage
lass who masticates mistrust until the penitent
recants? Swollen like a glommed leaf you wind
yourself, mildly mendicant, sympathetically
askew. Unless it's better to snarl than simper,
like silkworms mis-treed, or the strictest sigh.

# By Which I Promise

nothing you can put your finger on. Like
a digit in the dike or any needy hole. You
haven't reckoned with the alphabet, why
should you, whose job is always breaking
down & breaking down. There are names for
people more & less like you. There are sizes
which will never fit, although you squirm like
a champion. I may head for higher ground,
I may grind & bump & give the take to the
man on the street, but I won't forget your
inner life, that fine & twisted labyrinth.

# A New Leaf

Does this heavy lifting fray your seams? Do
you covet your neighbor's wings? These trees
grow blossoms of intoxicating sweetness,
milking melodies like Tuvan throat-songs or the
wavelengths of precious gems. Reptiles may smell
what you think, but I know your weight & breath,
your pain & depth. Worry not, your secret is safe
with me. Some say money heals the wounds it
must inflict. I say we have ourselves to blame for
what festers, like the bump & grind of microbes
& their better halves. Other options are abundant.
Hollow men & angry women know where I aspire.
Precocious babies too, although their lips are
sealed with basics. You'll never find my lies until
they quit. Who doesn't fail, from time to time,
from rank passivity? Why not linger in the past
as it brings us to the nowhere future? Sow what
you can't say, unpack those sea legs poised to pitch
& roll. Are those phaetons, or just lightning on
the horizon? Still the sky cannot cease groaning,
though I doubt it's ready to give up yet & go dark.

# How to Attempt or Enjoy

In which everyday pain nuzzles your neck &
other sundry accessories. While you may or may
not know whereof I speak. Trekking like Ulysses
to taste this shirking savor. Eyes closed, mind. Or
ambiguate. A lively intercourse of sodden factors,
*amour propre* & not-so-much, sorry victim of
that monster, success. To ignore the comedy of
horrors by which lively mortals swear. Which is to
say sacred & profane, above & beyond, laying the
buffet of options. Tasteless or spiked, extended or
ranged from here to there like anybody's flavored
dream. Or lose our windblown parts, *seriatim*.

# From the Outset,

the end goes on forever. With so much to lose & the fragrance of unmarked idylls to gain, we must fold our declinations & offer them to the moon-bullied waves. In one version we trade places with our former selves & resuscitate every which way until, weary of embellishment, you close your eyes & burrow towards the future. On the other hand, there must be alternates speculating on the porous shadow of gravity or the universe as data. In further iterations I will hum the pulse of your hair or sculpt the angle of your minstrel breath, while you draw studies in exploding sparks & wrestle my restless attention.

# ECLOGUE (I)

Beyond the personal evolution of desire, aroused by the heat of the world's gaze, the aftermath of the attack birthing confusion, threatening to consume your leaking heart. In the park, on a Sunday or any day but this one, afflictual. The sun flowing like honey. Skin humming like bees in the rippling heat, tempted to conflate the fecundity of flowers. You know what I'm thinking, you've been around this block before, chipped or not. Until the meal is over & we stuff ourselves like pillows dipped in sexy sauce. This despite the fug of complacence weighing us down, muddling our senses to pummeled zests. The answer is more of the same. The answer is (inaudible). Clogging our vesicles, clouding our fuddled wander, egging us on. Ditching us. Itching to wiggle our toes in the turbid terra. Until this twisted skin stirs the *je ne sais quoi* to allude or elude.

# ECLOGUE (II)

Hours like droplets, choices clamoring &
cluttering, tangled & nebulous, dispositive.
Disposed & indisposed. Or what, if not a
tattered pocket. Frayed as nerves. Afeared of
every outcome & its evil twin. On the wind the
latest news. On the wind the scent of death. On
the wind felicitation. The mountains turn their
high-boned cheeks on you, their son. They're
going through a rocky break-up (sings) *in the
valley below*. You mustn't think I don't want to
live for evermore. Want to want. Want to part-
ay. The organism makes the man. The organism
makes me. In the breeze eruption as unlikely as
any body's birth. Blowing in decision, indecision
showering you with shimmering regret.

# In Praise of Attention,

that stiff upper chamber of another bloody
pump. Or upper cut. Or cut to the quick
& the dead, to be blunt, to be smooth as an
animal in the grass, shooting the breeze with
its salutary moods, its whispering timbre.
Not so much chasing facsimilar euphoria as
synthesizing with the generative wisdom of
chlorophyll. Attending, nursing plus paying
out my bottomless cache, that recirculating
pump begging to be trimmed to droplets of
uncertainty, those nemeses of finitude. That *what
we observe is not nature itself but nature exposed
to our method of questioning.* Words grasping
boldly at the known grasping boldly at what is.

# In Praise of Mortality,

less something still & solid, amounting to,
achieved. Before the ashes. Until the. So
brightly small, so sharply silenced. Before the
closed book of now & now. After your turn
another, cruel & opaque. In which the gift of
beauty, cruel & opaque. That which I pretend/
cannot pretend. Tripping off the tongue of the
heart of the matter. That time is licking us for
lunch. While you, sweet snack, snapped off
at the stem, tape your wounds & struggle to
bridge the glistening gap. The caressing wind
whisking the brilliant minutes. Sun birthing &
burying, arming us for this minstrel fate. Let's
say I know what I am doing. Let's say I use this
sing-song voice, while you may or may not pay
tentative obeisance. The treasured chest squeezed
like a seed, bringing forth this dubious juice.

# In Praise of Indecision,

whether or not I want what you expect, in kind
or its evil twin. With or without your flattering
demands upon my appetite. In the carousel of
life, every lap a golden ring robbed from the rest,
unable to retry. Or strive to convert you, currently
sucking both alternating & direct as is your wont,
you red-blooded Americano you. Meanwhile, I
waffle. There may be this roof beneath our feet
but we are teetering, in search of liar ground. For
stability we should sway, for ability we should pray,
for mobility we should stay this baffling course.
Honk if you know (inaudible). By our fruits shall
they know us, which might be to love us, unless.

# Notes

"False Promise": Reference is made to Keats's theory of negative capability, "La Belle Dame Sans Merci," and hops (a bine).

"Four Shortcuts to Amelioration": C.f. Sigmund Freud's *Civilization and Its Discontents*.

"Another Chance": C.f. Aimé Césaire's founding role in Négritude, and his use of the famous line from Apollinaire's prose poem "Zone" to title his second book of poetry, *Soleil Cou Coupé*.

"In Praise of Efficiency": C.f. wave/particle duality, quantum superposition, and Einstein's objection that "God does not play dice with the universe."

"Words Dying Off": Reference is made to writings by George Berkeley and William Fossett on the "tree falls in the forest" thought experiment, as well as Andy Warhol's immortal remark about the transience of fame.

"This Is When": Reference is made to Sukey Tawdry, a character in *The Threepenny Opera*.

"Eclogue (II)": The italicized fragment is from "One More Cup of Coffee (Valley Below)" by Bob Dylan.

"In Praise of Attention": The italicized quotation is from Werner Heisenberg's *Physics and Philosophy: The Revolution in Modern Science* (1958).

# About the Author

Susan Lewis is the author of *Heisenberg's Salon* (BlazeVOX [books], 2017), *This Visit* (BlazeVOX [books], 2015), and *How to be Another* (Červená Barva Press, 2014), as well as the chapbooks *State of the Union* (Spuyten Duyvil Press, 2014), *The Following Message* (White Knuckle Press, 2013), *At Times Your Lines* (Argotist Ebooks, 2012), *Some Assembly Required* (Dancing Girl Press, 2011), *Commodity Fetishism,* winner of the 2009 Červená Barva Press Chapbook Award, and *Animal Husbandry* (Finishing Line Press, 2008).

Her work has been published in *The Awl, Berkeley Poetry Review, Boston Review, The Brooklyn Rail, The Journal, The New Orleans Review, Raritan, Seneca Review, Verse, Verse Daily, VOLT,* and many other journals and anthologies.

Lewis received her B.A. and her J.D. from U.C. Berkeley, and her M.F.A. from Sarah Lawrence College. She lives in New York City and is the editor and publisher of *Posit,* an online journal of literature and art (positjournal.com). Find out more at www.susanlewis.net.

# About the Artist

Brenda Goodman's work has been exhibited in over 40 solo and 200 group shows in museums and galleries across the US, including the Whitney Biennial. Her work has been reviewed in *Art in America, The New Yorker, The Detroit Free Press,* and *Huffington Post,* and is included in many collections, such as Agnes Gund, Santa Barbara Museum, and Detroit Institute of the Arts. She has received fellowships from the NEA and the NYFA, an Award for Exceptional Achievement from the American Academy of Arts and Letters, and an honorary doctorate from her alma mater, the College for Creative Studies. She lives and works in the Catskill Mountains. Find out more and see the full cover painting at www.brendagoodman.com.

# ABOUT THE WORD WORKS

The Word Works, a nonprofit literary organization, publishes contemporary poetry and presents public programs. Other imprints include The Washington Prize, International Editions, The Tenth Gate Prize, and the Hilary Tham Capital Collection. A reading period is also held in May.

Monthly, The Word Works offers free literary programs in the Chevy Chase, MD, Café Muse series, and each summer, it holds free poetry programs in Washington, D.C.'s Rock Creek Park. Annually in June, two high school students debut in the Joaquin Miller Poetry Series as winners of the Jacklyn Potter Young Poets Competition. Since 1974, Word Works programs have included: "In the Shadow of the Capitol," a symposium and archival project on the African American intellectual community in segregated Washington, D.C.; the Gunston Arts Center Poetry Series; the Poet Editor panel discussions at The Writer's Center; and Master Class workshops.

As a 501(c)3 organization, The Word Works has received awards from the National Endowment for the Arts, the National Endowment for the Humanities, the D.C. Commission on the Arts & Humanities, the Witter Bynner Foundation, Poets & Writers, The Writer's Center, Bell Atlantic, the David G. Taft Foundation, and others, including many generous private patrons.

The Word Works has established an archive of artistic and administrative materials in the Washington Writing Archive housed in the George Washington University Gelman Library. It is a member of the Council of Literary Magazines and Presses and its books are distributed by Small Press Distribution.

**wordworksbooks.org**

# THE WASHINGTON PRIZE

Nathalie Anderson, *Following Fred Astaire*, 1998

Michael Atkinson, *One Hundred Children Waiting for a Train*, 2001

Molly Bashaw, *The Whole Field Still Moving Inside It*, 2013

Carrie Bennett, *biography of water*, 2004

Peter Blair, *Last Heat*, 1999

John Bradley, *Love-in-Idleness: The Poetry of Roberto Zingarello*, 1995, 2ND edition 2014

Christopher Bursk, *The Way Water Rubs Stone*, 1988

Richard Carr, *Ace*, 2008

Jamison Crabtree, *Rel[AM]ent*, 2014

Jessica Cuello, *Hunt*, 2016

Barbara Duffey, *Simple Machines*, 2015

B. K. Fischer, *St. Rage's Vault*, 2012

Linda Lee Harper, *Toward Desire*, 1995

Ann Rae Jonas, *A Diamond Is Hard But Not Tough*, 1997

Susan Lewis, *Zoom*, 2017

Frannie Lindsay, *Mayweed*, 2009

Richard Lyons, *Fleur Carnivore*, 2005

Elaine Magarrell, *Blameless Lives*, 1991

Fred Marchant, *Tipping Point*, 1993, 2ND edition 2013

Ron Mohring, *Survivable World*, 2003

Barbara Moore, *Farewell to the Body*, 1990

Brad Richard, *Motion Studies*, 2010

Jay Rogoff, *The Cutoff*, 1994

Prartho Sereno, *Call from Paris*, 2007, 2ND edition 2013

Enid Shomer, *Stalking the Florida Panther*, 1987

John Surowiecki, *The Hat City After Men Stopped Wearing Hats*, 2006

Miles Waggener, *Phoenix Suites*, 2002

Charlotte Warren, *Gandhi's Lap*, 2000

Mike White, *How to Make a Bird with Two Hands*, 2011

Nancy White, *Sun, Moon, Salt*, 1992, 2ND edition 2010

George Young, *Spinoza's Mouse*, 1996

# THE HILARY THAM CAPITAL COLLECTION

Nathalie Anderson, *Stain*
Mel Belin, *Flesh That Was Chrysalis*
Carrie Bennett, *The Land Is a Painted Thing*
Doris Brody, *Judging the Distance*
Sarah Browning, *Whiskey in the Garden of Eden*
Grace Cavalieri, *Pinecrest Rest Haven*
Cheryl Clarke, *By My Precise Haircut*
Christopher Conlon, *Gilbert and Garbo in Love*
& *Mary Falls: Requiem for Mrs. Surratt*
Donna Denizé, *Broken like Job*
W. Perry Epes, *Nothing Happened*
David Eye, *Seed*
Bernadette Geyer, *The Scabbard of Her Throat*
Barbara G. S. Hagerty, *Twinzilla*
James Hopkins, *Eight Pale Women*
Donald Illich, *Chance Bodies*
Brandon Johnson, *Love's Skin*
Thomas March, *Aftermath*
Marilyn McCabe, *Perpetual Motion*
Judith McCombs, *The Habit of Fire*
James McEwen, *Snake Country*
Miles David Moore, *The Bears of Paris*
& *Rollercoaster*
Kathi Morrison-Taylor, *By the Nest*
Tera Vale Ragan, *Reading the Ground*
Michael Shaffner, *The Good Opinion of Squirrels*
Maria Terrone, *The Bodies We Were Loaned*
Hilary Tham, *Bad Names for Women*
& *Counting*
Barbara Ungar, *Charlotte Brontë, You Ruined My Life*
& *Immortal Medusa*
Jonathan Vaile, *Blue Cowboy*
Rosemary Winslow, *Green Bodies*
Michele Wolf, *Immersion*
Joe Zealberg, *Covalence*

THE TENTH GATE PRIZE

Jennifer Barber, *Works on Paper*, 2015
Lisa Lewis, *Taxonomy of the Missing*, 2017
Roger Sedarat, *Haji As Puppet*, 2016
Lisa Sewell, *Impossible Object*, 2014

INTERNATIONAL EDITIONS

Kajal Ahmad (Alana Marie Levinson-LaBrosse, Mewan Nahro Said Sofi
and Darya Abdul-Karim Ali Najin, trans., with Barbara Goldberg),
*Handful of Salt*
Keyne Cheshire (trans.), *Murder at Jagged Rock: A Tragedy by Sophocles*
Jeanette L. Clariond (Curtis Bauer, trans.), *Image of Absence*
Jean Cocteau (Mary-Sherman Willis, trans.), *Grace Notes*
Yoko Danno & James C. Hopkins, *The Blue Door*
Moshe Dor, Barbara Goldberg, Giora Leshem, eds.,
*The Stones Remember: Native Israeli Poets*
Moshe Dor (Barbara Goldberg, trans.), *Scorched by the Sun*
Lee Sang (Myong-Hee Kim, trans.), *Crow's Eye View:*
*The Infamy of Lee Sang, Korean Poet*
Vladimir Levchev (Henry Taylor, trans.), *Black Book of the Endangered Species*

## OTHER WORD WORKS BOOKS

Annik Adey-Babinski, *Okay Cool No Smoking Love Pony*
Karren L. Alenier, *Wandering on the Outside*
Karren L. Alenier, ed., *Whose Woods These Are*
Karren L. Alenier & Miles David Moore, eds.,
*Winners: A Retrospective of the Washington Prize*
Christopher Bursk, ed., *Cool Fire*
Willa Carroll, *Nerve Chorus*
Grace Cavalieri, *Creature Comforts*
Abby Chew, *A Bear Approaches from the Sky*
Barbara Goldberg, *Berta Broadfoot and Pepin the Short*
Akua Lezli Hope, *Them Gone*
Frannie Lindsay, *If Mercy*
Elaine Magarrell, *The Madness of Chefs*
Marilyn McCabe, *Glass Factory*
JoAnne McFarland, *Identifying the Body*
Kevin McLellan, *Ornitheology*
Leslie McGrath, *Feminists Are Passing from Our Lives*
Ann Pelletier, *Letter That Never*
Ayaz Pirani, *Happy You Are Here*
W.T. Pfefferle, *My Coolest Shirt*
Jacklyn Potter, Dwaine Rieves, Gary Stein, eds.,
*Cabin Fever: Poets at Joaquin Miller's Cabin*
Robert Sargent, *Aspects of a Southern Story*
*& A Woman from Memphis*
Miles Waggener, *Superstition Freeway*
Fritz Ward, *Tsunami Diorama*
Amber West, *Hen & God*
Nancy White, ed., *Word for Word*

CPSIA information can be obtained
at www.ICGtesting.com
Printed in the USA
FFOW02n1533230318
46016606-46930FF